To My Mother

TO MY MOTHER

Edited by Jill Wolf

ISBN 0-89954-682-X
Copyright © 1991 Antioch Publishing Company
Yellow Springs, Ohio 45387

Printed in Hong Kong through Bookbuilders Ltd

CONTENTS

*God can't be always everywhere; and, so,
Invented mothers.*
　　　　　　　—Sir Edwin Arnold

*All that I am, or hope to be, I owe to
my angel mother.*
　　　　　　　—Abraham Lincoln

Over my heart in the days that have flown,
No love like mother-love ever has shone...
—Elizabeth Akers Allen

And so because you love me, and because
I love you, Mother, I have woven a wreath
Of rhymes wherewith to crown your
honored name...
—Christina Rossetti

BLESSED ARE THE MOTHERS

God can't be always everywhere; and, so,
Invented mothers.

—*Sir Edwin Arnold*

When God thought of mother...so rich, so
deep, so divine, so full of soul, power and
beauty was the conception.

—*Henry Ward Beecher*

Mother is the name for God in the lips and
hearts of little children.

—*William Makepeace Thackeray*

The mother's face and voice are the first
conscious objects as the infant soul unfolds,
and she comes to stand in the very place of
God to her child.

—*Granville Stanley Hall*

The mother should consider herself as her child's sun, a changeless and ever radiant world whither the small restless creature, quick at tears and laughter, light, fickle, passionate, full of storms, may come for fresh stores of light, warmth, and electricity, of calm and of courage. The mother represents goodness, providence, law; that is, the divinity, under that form of it which is accessible to childhood.

—*Henri-Frédéric Amiel*

For Christ, who in the Virgin
Our motherhood has blest,
Is near to every woman
With a baby on her breast.

—*Mary Frances Butts*

"Whoever welcomes this little child in My
name welcomes Me; and whoever welcomes
Me welcomes the one who sent Me."

Luke 9:48 (NIV)

JUST AS A MOTHER

Just as a mother with sweet, pious face,
Yearns toward her little children from her seat,
Gives one a kiss, another an embrace,
Takes this upon her knees, that on her feet;
And while from actions, looks, complaints,
    pretenses,
She learns their feeling and their various will,
To this a look, to that a word dispenses,
And whether stern or smiling, loves them
    still—
So Providence for us, high, infinite,
Makes our necessities its watchful task,
Hearkens to all our prayers, helps all our wants,
And e'en if it denies what seems our right,
Either denies because 'twould have us ask,
Or seems but to deny, and in denying grants.

—*Leigh Hunt*

A mother is a mother still,
The holiest thing alive.
—*Samuel Taylor Coleridge*

My mother was an angel upon earth. She
was a minister of blessing to all human
beings within her sphere of action...but if
virtue alone is happiness below, never was
existence upon earth more blessed than hers.
—*John Quincy Adams*

A mother's prayers, silent and gentle, can
never miss the road to the throne of all bounty.
—*Henry Ward Beecher*

Blessed are the mothers of the earth, for they have combined the practical and the spiritual into one workable way of human life. They have darned little stockings, mended little dresses, washed little faces, and have pointed little eyes to the stars and little souls to eternal things.

—*William L. Stidger*

11

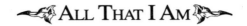

ALL THAT I AM

All that I am, or hope to be, I owe to my angel mother.

—Abraham Lincoln

The mother's heart is the child's schoolroom.

—Henry Ward Beecher

All I am I owe to my mother...I attribute all my success in life to the moral, intellectual, and physical education I received from her.

—George Washington

For my heart is wax to be moulded as she pleases, but enduring as marble to retain whatever impression she shall make upon it.

—Miguel de Cervantes

Oh, wondrous power! how little understood,
Entrusted to the mother's mind alone,
To fashion genius, form the soul for good,
Inspire a West, or train a Washington.

—Sarah Josepha Hale

For the hand that rocks the cradle
Is the hand that rules the world.

—William R. Wallace

One good mother is worth a hundred school masters.

—George Herbert

I think it must somewhere be written, that the virtues of the mothers shall be visited on their children...

—*Charles Dickens*

A mother has, perhaps, the hardest earthly lot. Yet no mother worth the name ever gave herself thoroughly for her child who did not feel that, after all, she reaped what she had sown.

—*Henry Ward Beecher*

The remembrance that my mother so loved
me and that she dedicated me to mankind;
the remembrance that it was her thought and
that it was the inspiration of her prayer that I
was to be set apart not to be a great man
myself, but to be connected with the welfare
of the human race—I have never lost the
inspiration of it, nor have I ceased to be
thankful to my mother, and to reverence her,
that she had such a thought and wish with
regard to me.

—*Henry Ward Beecher*

MY MOTHER

Who fed me from her gentle breast,
And hushed me in her arms to rest,
And on my cheek sweet kisses pressed?
                    My Mother.

When sleep forsook my open eye,
Who was it sang sweet lullaby,
And rocked me that I should not cry?
                    My Mother.

Who sat and watched my infant head,
When sleeping on my cradle bed,
And tears of sweet affection shed?
                    My Mother.

When pain and sickness made me cry,
Who gazed upon my heavy eye,
And wept for fear that I should die?
                    My Mother.

Who dressed my doll in clothes so gay,
And taught me pretty how to play,
And minded all I had to say?
My Mother.

Who ran to help me when I fell,
And would some pretty story tell,
Or kiss the place to make it well?
My Mother.

Who taught my infant lips to pray,
And love God's holy book and day,
And walk in wisdom's pleasant way?
My Mother.

And can I ever cease to be,
Affectionate and kind to thee,
Who was so very kind to me?
My Mother.

Ah! no, the thought I cannot bear,
And if God please my life to spare,
I hope I shall reward thy care,
                    My Mother.

When thou art feeble, old and gray,
My healthy arms shall be thy stay,
And I will soothe thy pains away,
                    My Mother.

And when I see thee hang thy head,
'Twill be my turn to watch thy bed,
And tears of sweet affection shed,
                    My Mother.

For God, who lives above the skies,
Would look with vengeance in His eyes,
If I should ever dare despise
                    My Mother.

—*Jane Taylor*

My mother's influence in molding my character was conspicuous. She forced me to learn daily long chapters of the Bible by heart. To that discipline and patient, accurate resolve I owe not only much of my general power of taking pains, but the best part of my taste for literature.

—John Ruskin

An ounce of mother is worth a pound of clergy.

—Spanish Proverb

I remember my mother's prayers; they have clung to me all my life.

—Abraham Lincoln

We search the world for truth; we cull the
 good, the pure, the beautiful
From graven stone and written scroll, from
 all old flower-fields of the soul.
And, weary seekers of the best, we come
 back laden from our quest,
To find that all the sages said is in the book
 our Mothers read.

—John Greenleaf Whittier

TO MY MOTHER

If e'er for human bliss or woe
I feel the sympathetic glow;
If e'er my heart has learn'd to know
The gen'rous wish or prayer;
Who sow'd the germ with tender hand?
Who mark'd its infant leaves expand?
My mother's fostering care.

And if one flower of charms refined
May grace the garden of my mind;
'Twas she who nursed it there:
She loved to cherish and adorn
Each blossom of the soil;
To banish every weed and thorn,
That oft opposed her toil!

—*Felicia Hemans*

MY MOTHER DEAR

There was a place in childhood that I
    remember well,
And there was a voice of sweetest tone
    bright fairy tales did tell:
And gentle words and fond embrace were
    given with joy to me
When I was in that happy place, upon my
    Mother's knee.

When fairy tales were ended, "Good night,"
    she softly said,
And kissed and laid me down to sleep within
    my tiny bed;
And holy words she taught me there—
    methinks I yet can see
Her angel eyes, as close I knelt beside my
    Mother's knee.

In sickness of my childhood, the perils of
    my prime,
The sorrows of my riper years, the cares of
    every time;
When doubt and danger weighed me down,
    the pleading all for me,
It was a fervent prayer to Heaven that bent
    my Mother's knee.

—*Samuel Lover*

Stories first heard at a mother's knee are never wholly forgotten—a little spring that never quite dries up in our journey through scorching years.

—*Giovanni Ruffini*

His sweetest dreams were still of that dear voice that soothed his infancy.

—*Robert Southey*

MY TRUST

A picture memory brings to me:
I look across the years and see
Myself beside my mother's knee.

I feel her gentle hand restrain
My selfish moods, and know again
A child's blind sense of wrong and pain.

But wiser now, a man gray grown,
My childhood's needs are better known,
My mother's chastening love I own.

—John Greenleaf Whittier

An Enduring Love

Maternal love: a miraculous substance
which God multiplies as He divides it.

—*Victor Hugo*

No language can express the power and
beauty and heroism and majesty of a
mother's love. It shrinks not where man
cowers, and grows stronger where man
faints, and over the wastes of worldly fortune
sends the radiance of quenchless fidelity like
a star in heaven.

—*Edwin H. Chapin*

There is in all this cold and hollow world no fount of deep, strong, deathless love, save that within a mother's heart.

—Felicia Hemans

One lamp—thy mother's love—amid the stars
Shall lift its pure flame changeless, and before
The throne of God, burn through eternity—
Holy—as it was lit and lent thee here.

—Nathaniel P. Willis

There is a religion in all deep love, but the love of a mother is the veil of a softer light between the heart and the heavenly Father.

—Samuel Taylor Coleridge

A mother's love—how sweet the name!
What is a mother's love?
A noble, pure, and tender flame,
Enkindled from above,
To bless a heart of earthly mold;
The warmest love that can grow cold:
This is a mother's love.

—*J. Montgomery*

Oh, the love of a mother, love which none can forget.

—Victor Hugo

Her first ministration for her infant is to enter, as it were, the valley of the shadow of death, and win its life at the peril of her own. How different must an affection thus founded be from all others!

—Lydia Sigourney

If there be aught surpassing human deed or word or thought, it is a mother's love.

—Marchioness de Spadara

There is no love like the good old love—the love that mother gave us.

—Eugene Field

Among human relations, the love of a good mother for her offspring, is in a class by itself. In other words, it is unique, especially unique in fact. Unique because there is nothing else like it in this big world in which we all live and have our being. Especially unique because it is ever-trustful, ever-devoted, ever-forgiving, ever-tender, ever-unchanging, ever-enduring.

—*Samuel Johnson*

Over my heart in the days
    that have flown,
No love like mother-love
    ever has shone;
No other worship
    abides and endures,
Faithful, unselfish,
    and patient, like yours.
    —*Elizabeth Akers Allen*

But a mother's love endures through all; in good repute, in bad repute, in the face of the world's condemnation, a mother still loves on, and still hopes...still she remembers the infant smiles that once filled her bosom with rapture, the merry laugh, the joyful shout of his childhood, the opening promise of his youth; and she can never be brought to think him all unworthy.

—*Washington Irving*

Who is it that loves me and will love me
forever with an affection which no chance,
no misery, no crime of mine can do away?
It is you, my mother.

—Thomas Carlyle

The greatest happiness of life is the
conviction that we are loved, loved for
ourselves, or rather, loved in spite of
ourselves.

—Victor Hugo

Youth fades; love droops; the leaves of
   friendship fall:
A mother's secret hope outlives them all.

—Oliver Wendell Holmes

A mother's love is indeed the golden link that binds youth to age; and he is still but a child, however time may have furrowed his cheek or silvered his brow, who can yet recall, with softened heart, the fond devotion, or the gentle tidings, of the best friend that God ever gives us.

—*Christian Bovee*

Children, look in those eyes, listen to that dear voice, notice the feeling of even a single touch that is bestowed upon you by that gentle hand! Make much of it while yet you have that most precious of all good gifts, a loving mother. Read the unfathomable love of those eyes; the kind anxiety of that tone and look, however slight your pain. In after life you may have friends, fond, dear friends, but never will you have again the inexpressible love and gentleness lavished upon you, which none but a mother can bestow.

—*Thomas Babington Macaulay*

A mother is the truest friend we have, when trials, heavy and sudden fall upon us; when adversity takes the place of prosperity; when friends who rejoice with us in our sunshine desert us, when trouble thickens around us, still will she cling to us, and endeavor by her kind precepts and counsels to dissipate the clouds of darkness, and cause peace to return to our hearts.

—*Washington Irving*

The tie which links mother and child is of such pure and immaculate strength as to be never violated, except by those whose feelings are withered by vitiated society. Holy, simple, and beautiful in its construction, it is the emblem of all we can imagine of fidelity and truth.

—*Washington Irving*

IN PRAISE OF MOTHER

What is better than gold?
Jasper.
What is better than jasper?
Wisdom.
What is better than wisdom?
Women.
And what is better than a good woman?
Nothing.

—Geoffrey Chaucer

Honor women! They entwine and weave
heavenly roses in our earthly life.

—*Johann von Schiller*

To the man who has had a mother, all women
are sacred for her sake.

—*Jean Paul Richter*

Every man, for the sake of the great blessed
Mother in Heaven, and for the love of his
own little mother on earth, should handle all
womankind gently, and hold them in all honor.

—*Alfred, Lord Tennyson*

She is clothed with strength and dignity; she can laugh at the days to come. She speaks with wisdom, and faithful instruction is on her tongue. She watches over the affairs of her household and does not eat the bread of idleness. Her children arise and call her blessed; her husband also, and he praises her: "Many women do noble things, but you surpass them all." Charm is deceptive and beauty is fleeting; but a woman who fears the Lord is to be praised. Give her the reward she has earned, and let her works bring her praise at the city gate.

Proverbs 31: 25-31 (NIV)

There is an angel in the family, who, with a mysterious influence of charm, sweetness and love, makes the accomplishment of duties less arduous, pains less bitter. The angel of the family is the woman. Mother, Wife, Sister. Woman is the caress of life, the gentleness of love.

—*Guiseppe Mazzini*

...I feel that, in the Heavens above,
The angels, whispering to one another,
Can find, among their burning terms of love,
None so devotional as that of "Mother"...

—*Edgar Allan Poe*

Ere on my bed my limbs I lay,
God grant me grace my prayers to say!
O God, preserve my mother dear
In health and strength for many a year.

—*Samuel Taylor Coleridge*

Lord who ordainst for mankind
Benignant toils and tender cares,
We thank Thee for the ties that bind
The mother to the child she bears.

—*William Cullen Bryant*

The many make the household,
But only one the home.

—*James Russell Lowell*

MOTHER

The spirit of home is Mother.
The charm of her love is there.
One knows the joy of her presence
And her ever tender care.

Friendships will sometimes vary,
The old are changed for the new.
But always the same dear Mother
Will gladden a lifetime through!

—*Author Unknown*

Where there is a mother in the house, matters speed well.

—*Bronson Alcott*

Most of all the other beautiful things in life come by twos and threes, by dozens and hundreds. Plenty of roses, stars, sunsets, rainbows, brothers and sisters, aunts and cousins, but only one mother in the whole world.

—*Kate Douglas Wiggin*

Hundreds of stars in the pretty sky,
Hundreds of shells on the shore together,
Hundreds of birds that go singing by,
Hundreds of birds in the sunny weather,
Hundreds of dewdrops to greet the dawn,
Hundreds of bees in the purple clover,
Hundreds of butterflies on the lawn,
But only *one mother* the wide world over.

—*George Cooper*

There is no velvet so soft as mother's lap, no rose so lovely as her smile, no path so flowery as that imprinted with her footsteps.

—Archbishop Thomson

Is not a young mother one of the sweetest sights life shows us?

—William Makepeace Thackeray

Mother's arms are made of tenderness, and sweet sleep blesses the child who lies therein.

—Victor Hugo

...there is one picture so beautiful that no painter has ever been able perfectly to reproduce it, and that is the picture of the mother holding in her arms her babe.

—William Jennings Bryan

A MOTHER'S PICTURE

She seemed an angel to our infant eyes!
Once, when the glorifying moon revealed
Her who at evening by our pillow kneeled—
Soft-voiced and golden-haired, from holy
   skies
Flown to her loves on wings of Paradise—
We looked to see the pinions half-concealed.
The Tuscan vines and olives will not yield
Her back to me, who loved her in this wise,
And since have little known her, but have
   grown
To see another mother, tenderly,
Watch over sleeping darlings of her own;
Perchance the years have changed her: yet
   alone
This picture lingers: still she seems to me
The fair, young Angel of my infancy.

                  —Edmund Clarence Stedman

MY MOTHER

The sweetest face in all the world to me,
Set in a frame of shining silver hair,
With eyes whose language is fidelity;
This is my mother. Is she not most fair?

O Mother! In the changeful years now flown,
Since, as a child, I leant upon your knee,
Life has not brought to me, nor fortune shown,
Such tender love! Such yearning sympathy!

Let fortune smile or frown, whiche'er she will,
It matters not, I scorn her fickle ways!
I never shall be quite bereft until
I lose my mother's honest blame and praise!

—May Riley Smith

A MOTHER'S PICTURE

"A lady, the loveliest ever the sun looked
    down upon,
You must paint for me.
O, if I could only make you see
The clear blue eyes, the tender smile,
The sovereign sweetness, the gentle grace,
The woman's soul, and the angel's face,
That are beaming on me all the while,
But I need not speak these foolish words;
One word tells you all I would say,
She is my mother: and you will agree
That all the rest may be thrown away."

—*Alice Cary*

As pure and sweet, her fair brow seemed
    eternal as the sky;
And like the brook's low song her voice, a
    sound which could not die.
Sweet promptings unto kindest deeds were
    in her very look;
We read her face, as one who reads a true
    and holy book.

—*John Greenleaf Whittier*

HER HANDS

My mother's hands are cool and fair,
They can do anything.
Delicate mercies hide them there
Like flowers in the spring.

When I was small and could not sleep,
She used to come to me,
And with my cheek upon her hand
How sure my rest would be.

For everything she ever touched
Of beautiful or fine,
Their memories living in her hands
Would warm that sleep of mine.

—Anna Hempstead Branch

TRIBUTE TO A MOTHER

Faith that withstood the shocks of toil and
    time;
Hope that defied despair;
Patience that conquered care;
And loyalty, whose courage was sublime;
The great deep heart that was a home for
    all—
Just, eloquent, and strong
In protest against wrong;
Wide charity, that knew no sin, no fall;
The Spartan spirit that made life so grand,
Mating poor daily needs
With high, heroic deeds,
That wrested happiness from Fate's hard
    hand.

—Louisa May Alcott

TO MOTHER

Sonnets are full of love, and this my tome
Has many sonnets: so here now shall be
One sonnet more, a love sonnet, from me
To her whose heart is my heart's quiet home.
To my first love, my Mother, on whose knee
I learnt love-lore that is not troublesome;
Whose service is my special dignity,
And she my lodestar while I go and come.

And so because you love me, and because
I love you, Mother, I have woven a wreath
Of rhymes wherewith to crown your
    honored name:
In you not fourscore years can dim the flame
Of love, whose blessed glow transcends the
    laws
Of time and change and mortal life and
    death.

—Christina Rossetti

TO MY MOTHER

They tell us of an Indian tree
Which howsoe'er the sun and sky
May tempt its boughs to wander free,
And shoot and blossom, wide and high,
Far better loves to bend its arms
Downward again to that dear earth
From which the life, that fills and warms
Its grateful being, first had birth.
'Tis thus, though wooed by flattering friends,
And fed with fame (if fame it be),
This heart, my own dear mother, bends,
With love's true instinct, back to thee!

—Thomas Moore

TO MOTHER

I hope that soon, dear mother,
You and I may be
In the quiet room my fancy
Has so often made for thee—
The pleasant sunny chamber,
The cushioned easy-chair,
The book laid for your reading,
The vase of flowers fair;
The desk beside the window,
Where the sun shines warm and bright:
And there in ease and quiet
The promised book you write;
While I sit close beside you,
Content at last to see
That you can rest, dear mother,
And I can cherish thee.

—Louisa May Alcott